GUESS MY TALENT?

Donald Gorbach

Copyright © 2017 by Donald Gorbach

All rights reserved.

ISBN-10 1979442797
ISBN-13 978-1979442794

"GETTING PEOPLE TO LIKE YOU FOR YOU…
THAT'S MY TALENT."

—KIM KARDASHIAN

REALITYCOVERBOOKS.COM

www.ingramcontent.com/pod-product-compliance
Lightning Source LLC
Chambersburg PA
CBHW050214230526
45470CB00001B/374